HOW SMART IS YOUR
DOG?

Test your pet's IQ

First published by Parragon in 2012

Parragon
Queen Street House
4 Queen Street
Bath BA1 1HE, UK

www.parragon.com

Created by Tall Tree Ltd
Editor: Jon Richards
Designer: Ed Simkins
Consultant: Jon Peplow MBIPDT

Cover design by Andrew Easton, Ummagumma

ISBN 978-1-4454-6584-5

Printed in Indonesia

HOW SMART IS YOUR DOG?

Test your pet's IQ

PaRragon

Bath • New York • Singapore • Hong Kong • Cologne • Delhi
Melbourne • Amsterdam • Johannesburg • Auckland • Shenzhen

Contents

Introduction

You might think that your dog is one clever canine – but how can you prove it? Well, this book is designed to put your pooch through its paces.

The tests in this book are designed to see how your dog reacts to the world around it and to you, its owner. Does it take instructions well or does it choose not to hear you? Will it respect your property or do you dread opening the door, expecting to find doggy destruction?

We'll now hand you over to our very own "guide dog", Rufus, who will take you by the paw.

Leader of the pack

If you're after the perfect pooch or the craftiest canine, then look no further than these breeds. I'd like to think that I'd be top of the pile, but then I'm not one to boast.

German Shepherd

Dogs have been used by humans to hunt and as pets for more than 12,000 years.

This is no dumb dog and German Shepherds are used in a wide variety of roles, including guard dogs and guide dogs, as well as working in the police and the military – something of a jack of all trades.

3

There are now more than 400 different breeds of dog, from Great Danes to Chihuahuas.

Border Collie

The Einstein of the canine world, the Border Collie is used to herd sheep and can understand and act on a number of commands, including various shouts and different whistles.

1

... and the rest

4. Golden Retriever
5. Doberman Pinscher
6. Shetland Sheepdog
7. Labrador Retriever
8. Papillon
9. Rottweiler
10. Australian Cattle Dog
11. Pembroke Welsh Corgi
12. Miniature Schnauzer
13. English Springer Spaniel

14. Belgian Shepherd Tervuren
15. Schipperke
15. Belgian Sheepdog
17. Collie
17. Keeshond
19. German Shorthaired Pointer
20. Flat-Coated Retriever
20. English Cocker Spaniel
20. Standard Schnauzer
23. Brittany

Poodle

Not much of a working dog, but clever all the same. So much so that some people have bred the poodle with other breeds to make them more intelligent, creating Labradoodles, Schnoodles and Pekepoos!

2

Could do better?

These dogs might not be the top of the class, but they still make lovable pets. Just don't expect them to get things right all of the time!

Q: What dog loves to take baths?

A: A sham-poodle

Bulldog

This is one breed of dog that's going to struggle in a beauty pageant AND an intelligence test! Even so, bulldogs are known to be gentle, reliable and ferociously loyal to their owners.

3

Afghan Hound

This breed of dog has been described as "noble", "regal" and "aristocratic". It's a shame then that its intellect cannot match its royal appearance.

1

2

Basenji

An ancient hunting dog from central Africa, this breed is also known as the "barkless dog". As the name suggests, you won't get any "ruff" treatment from this dog, but watch out as its bite is probably worse than its bark.

Super dogs on screen

Lights, camera, action! These performing pooches know how to put on a star turn, bringing a smile to the face or a tear to the eye with the slightest twitch of a tail.

Discovered by a soldier in a bombed-out building in France during World War I, Rin Tin Tin starred in some 20 movies. His children and grandchildren have carried on the Rin Tin Tin name since his death in 1932.

Only three dogs have stars on the Hollywood Walk of Fame – Rin Tin Tin, Lassie and Strongheart.

For me, the star of the 1939 movie *The Wizard of Oz* was Toto, played by a Cairn Terrier called Terry. As a reward for her stunning performance, Terry was paid more than some of the human actors! She went on to appear in another 13 movies.

Originally played by a Rough Collie called Pal, the character of Lassie has appeared in movies, on radio and even had its own long-running TV show. *Variety* even called Lassie one of the "100 icons of all time"!

The story goes that Rin Tin Tin signed the contracts for all of his movies himself – using a paw print.

13

Helpful hints

🐾 Your dog should enjoy carrying out these exercises as it will think you are playing rather than testing it.

🐾 If your dog should show some signs of distress or becoming agitated, stop the exercises immediately.

🐾 Don't feel you have to complete all of the tests in one go – spread them out over a few days to maximize the fun.

Test time

The simple tests at the start of this sequence will explore your dog's character, while the more difficult exercises later on will really test its intelligence and ability to solve problems. Keep track of the score by ticking the boxes next to each exercise to show how your dog performed.

Sometimes life can put a pooch in some strange situations. Does your dog pay attention, or simply roll over?

When put in this new environment, does your dog:

1 Take your dog to a nice, quiet place that it has never been to before. This should be a safe spot where it can't run away, such as a garden.

2 See how your dog reacts when you let it off the lead.

 Explore every single square inch? **5 points**

 Start to explore, but loses interest after a short time? **4 points**

 Explore the garden cautiously? **3 points**

 Stay by your side, but looks around? **2 points**

 Go to sleep? **1 point**

New sounds

What's that sound? Could it be a tasty postman, or a new toy to play with?

1 Get hold of something that makes a sound your dog hasn't heard before, such as a bicycle horn or a rattle.

2 Wait until your dog is relaxed and even lying down. Then make the sound, suddenly and loudly.

3 Record how your dog reacts.

Does your dog:

 Get up and try to find the sound? **5 points**

 Get up, look around and then lie down again? **4 points**

 Raise its head and look about? **3 points**

 Lift its ears? **2 points**

 Not react at all? **1 point**

You can spend hours in front of a mirror trying to look your best, but how does your dog treat its reflection?

1 Place a mirror on the floor (propped up against a wall if necessary), so that your dog can see itself.

2 Draw your dog's attention to the mirror so that it comes up to take a look.

3 Record how your dog reacts.

When your dog sees its reflection, does it:

 Get excited at the new playmate it sees? **5 points**

 Have a sniff before walking away? **4 points**

 Wag its tail, but soon loses interest? **3 points**

 Sniff the mirror, but doesn't look at the reflection? **2 points**

 Walk away without paying any attention? **1 point**

Suitcase

Everyone likes a good holiday, but how does pooch react when you break out the cases?

When it sees the case, does the dog:

 Become excited, having linked the case to a new event?
5 points

 Sniff and explore the case in detail?
4 points

 Explore the case for a short time?
3 points

 Lift its head to look at the case?
2 points

 Ignore the case completely?
1 point

1 Dig out a suitcase (a nice large one that your dog doesn't see all that often), and place it by the front door, with your dog watching.

2 Record how your dog reacts to this strange new object.

Squeaking

Life would be dull without a squeaky toy to chew on. But what if pooch can hear the toy and not see it?

1 Hold a squeaky toy behind your back so that your dog can't see it.

2 Start squeaking.

3 See how your dog reacts to this new sound.

When the squeaks start, does it:

Realize the squeaks are coming from behind you?
5 points

Stand in front of you wagging its tail?
4 points

Appear confused?
3 points

Lift its head for a short time?
2 points

Not react at all?
1 point

Speaking

Our speech might be a bit "ruff", but we know what you're saying – most of the time. Try your pet out with a few new words.

When you start calling out, does your dog:

1 Wait until your dog is nice and relaxed and when it's not time for its walkies.

2 Start calling out a random word (such as "television"), but using the same tone of voice you would for "walkies" (nice and excited).

✓ Lie still and not react?
5 points

Lift its head to investigate?
4 points

Stand up, but look confused?
3 points

Walk over to you to investigate?
2 points

Get excited as if it's going on a walk?
1 point

Tickle time

Up a bit, down a bit, left a bit, ahhh, just there! Every dog likes to be tickled.

When you start to tickle, does your dog:

1 Wait until your dog is nice and relaxed.

2 Start to tickle your dog behind its ear.

3 Record how your dog reacts.

 Lift its head to get a better tickle?
5 points

 Shake its head?
3 points

 Wag its tail, but doesn't do anything else?
4 points

 Fail to react at all?
2 points

 Pull its head away?
1 point

Life is always putting little obstacles in your path, but some of us deal with them better than others.

1 With your dog on a lead, walk it down a short pathway.

2 Now place some small sticks on the path and lead your dog along it again. Record how your dog reacts to these obstacles.

On the second run, does your dog:

 Step over all the sticks, without touching any?
5 points

 Touch the first few sticks, but clear the rest?
4 points

 Knock most of the sticks, but clear the last few?
3 points

 Knock all the sticks?
2 points

 Refuse to walk near the sticks?
1 point

I don't know about you, but I'm a creature of habit. When you gotta go, you gotta go!

1 Wait until your dog is nice and relaxed and it is not time for its walk.

2 Calmly and quietly pick up your house keys and the dog's lead as if you're going on a walk.

3 Watch how your dog reacts.

When you pick up the lead, does your dog:

 Get up straight away and become excited? **5 points**

 Get up, but only when you head for the door? **4 points**

 Get up, but looks a little confused? **3 points**

 Lift its head, but does not get up? **2 points**

 Not react at all? **1 point**

When is a treat not a treat? When it's not in my stomach! How does your canine chum react to this tricky test?

1 Hold a treat out in front of your dog.

2 Making sure you've got your dog's full attention, pretend to eat the treat.

3 Watch how your pet reacts.

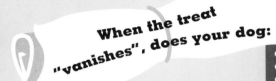

When the treat "vanishes", does your dog:

 Check your hand to see if it's still there? **5 points**

 Search for the missing treat? **4 points**

 Watch you as if you've eaten the treat? **3 points**

 Walk away, thinking the treat has gone? **2 points**

 Pay no attention at all? **1 point**

I can get past any obstacle that's put in my way – but a little help now and again is always appreciated.

When you call its name, does your dog:

1 Put your dog on one side of a high barrier, such as a fence, and tell it to stay (you may need a friend to hold the dog in place).

2 Walk to the other side of the barrier and call your dog's name.

3 Watch how your dog reacts.

 Run up and down the fence, trying to find a way around? **5 points**

 Try to squeeze through any tiny gap? **4 points**

 Try to jump over the fence, even though it can't? **3 points**

 Stay still and wait to be lifted over? **2 points**

 Run off in a different direction? **1 point**

No one likes a door shut in their face, but what happens if you have to get to the other side?

1 Put your dog outside through the back door and close it.

2 Call your dog's name.

3 Watch how your pet reacts.

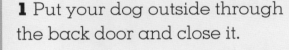
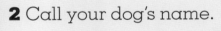

When you call its name, does it:

Run around to another door that's open? **5 points**

Bark to be let in? **4 points**

Run backwards and forwards looking confused? **3 points**

Jump up and down and look keen to get in? **2 points**

Not move from the spot? **1 point**

All in a day's work

It's a dog's life working all day, every day. But we understand that there are some things we dogs can do that you humans just don't have the equipment for.

Some breeds of dog have 50 times more smell receptors in their noses than humans.

With a nose as sensitive as ours, it's no surprise that we can put it to good use finding bad things. Sniffer dogs are used to hunt for everything from drugs to explosives.

A calm temperament is needed to help people out. Labradors and German Shepherds are perfect as guide dogs for the blind, while other breeds can help people who are hard of hearing.

A sensitive nose and a fearless attitude are perfect for hunting for people trapped under a collapsed building. Rescue dogs like these have saved thousands of lives.

It's always good fun telling other animals what to do and where to go, and these guys get to do it all day long. Dogs are used to herd all sorts of animals, including sheep, cows and even geese!

A dog's ears are controlled by 18 muscles, allowing them to move the ears towards a sound so they can hear it better.

What you need

* Treat
* Timer
* Can

Getting food is hard work at the best of times, but hiding it under a can really makes me hot under the collar!

> **Q: What do you call a college qualification for dogs?**
>
> **A: A pe-degree**

1 Show the dog a treat.

2 Have the dog sit and stay (someone may hold the dog if necessary).

3 With the dog's full attention, slowly place the treat on the floor and cover it with the can.

4 Start the timer and encourage the dog to get the treat.

If the dog pushes the can aside and gets the food in:

✓ 5 seconds or less
5 points

30 to 59 seconds
3 points

6 to 29 seconds
4 points

More than 60 seconds
2 points

If the dog makes no effort to get the treat
1 point

What you need

🐾 Treat

🐾 Timer

🐾 Small towel

This one will really stretch your canine's creative talents – can it make that treat disappear or will it be as sick as a dog?!

> **Q: Who is a dog's favourite composer?**
>
> **A: Pooch-ini**

1 Show the dog a treat.

2 Have the dog sit and stay (someone may hold the dog if necessary).

3 Place the treat on the floor and cover it with the towel.

4 Start the timer and encourage the dog to get the treat.

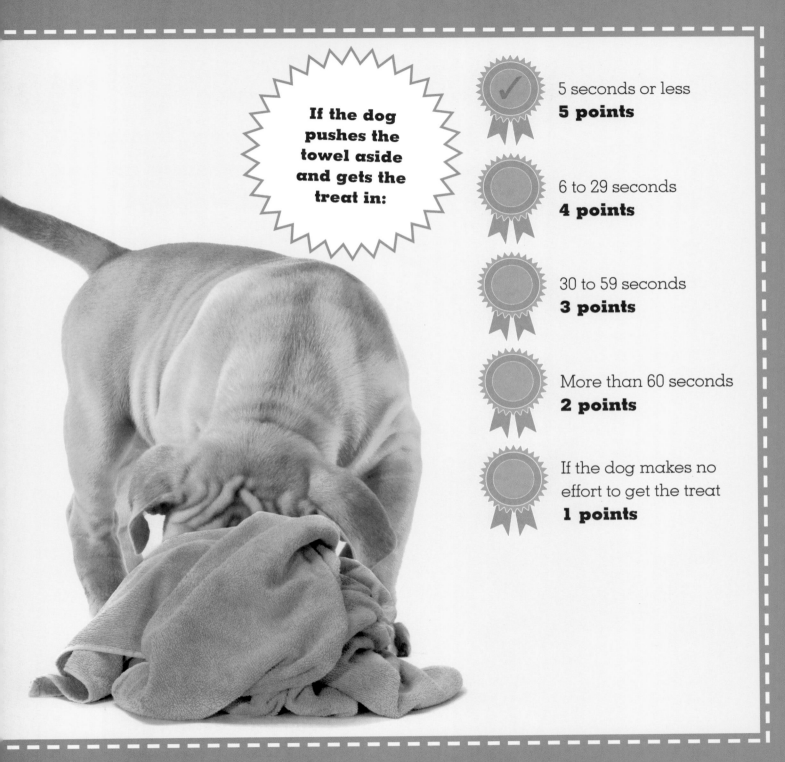

If the dog pushes the towel aside and gets the treat in:

5 seconds or less
5 points

6 to 29 seconds
4 points

30 to 59 seconds
3 points

More than 60 seconds
2 points

If the dog makes no effort to get the treat
1 points

Changing rooms

Just when you find your favourite spot, someone moves things around – where am I meant to sleep?

> **Instead of just moving the furniture around, try swapping some of it with furniture from a different room as well.**

1 Ask someone to take your dog out for a walk.

2 While your dog is out of the house, move the furniture around in the dog's favourite room.

3 Start the timer and see how your dog reacts when it comes back into the room.

When your dog enters the room, does it:

 Start to explore the whole room straight away? **5 points**

 Start to explore after 15 seconds? **4 points**

 Start to explore after 30 seconds? **3 points**

 Look confused and stay by your side? **2 points**

 Lie down and ignore the changes? **1 point**

What you need

🐾 Large bath towel

🐾 Timer

Most of us long to be free to sniff trees and bark at cars, while others just like to snooze in a nice, quiet, dark place.

1 Your dog should be awake and reasonably active.

2 Let the dog sniff the towel.

3 With a smooth movement, throw the towel over the dog's head, so its head and shoulders are completely covered (you may want to practise this without the dog first). Start timing and watch silently.

If the dog frees itself in:

 5 seconds or less
5 points

 6 to 14 seconds
4 points

 15 to 29 seconds
3 points

 30 to 59 seconds
2 points

 If the dog hasn't freed itself after 60 seconds
1 point

Use the right towel for the job – too small, and pooch will be free in no time. Too big, and it might get stuck!

We all like a happy owner. Just make sure you brush your teeth before you smile.

What you need

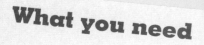

🐾 A big smile

1 Put your dog about 2 metres away from you.

2 Don't tell your dog to stay or sit.

3 Stare at your dog's face, wait for about four seconds and then smile broadly. Make a note of how your dog reacts.

Q: What do you call a dog that inherits a fortune?

A: An Heir-dale

When you smile, does your dog:

 Come to you straight away, wagging its tail? **5 points**

 Move towards you slowly? **4 points**

 Wag its tail but doesn't move? **3 points**

 Walk away? **2 points**

 Pay no attention at all? **1 point**

What you need

🐾 Two treats

Can your dog complete this short-term memory test in double-quick time, or does it have to "paws" for thought?

You can also use a timer to see how quickly your pooch finds the treats.

1 Hold your dog by the collar.

2 Throw the treats to opposite sides of a room.

3 After counting to four, let go of your dog and make a note of how it reacts.

When you let go of your dog, does it:

 Find both treats easily? **5 points**

 Find the first treat, but takes a while to find the second? **4 points**

 Find the first treat, but fails to find the second? **3 points**

 Fail to find either treat? **2 points**

 Not move at all? **1 point**

What you need

🐾 Treat

🐾 Timer

I like to think I've got a very good memory and would pass these tests easily. Now, where did I put my owner... ?

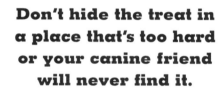

Don't hide the treat in a place that's too hard or your canine friend will never find it.

1 Make your dog sit (or ask a friend to hold its collar).

2 With your dog watching, hide the treat.

3 After a count of five, encourage the dog to find the treat (or let go of its collar) and start the timer.

When you let go, does your dog:

Go straight to the treat? **5 points**

Find the treat in 45 seconds? **3 points**

Find the treat in 15 seconds? **4 points**

Fail to find the treat? **2 points**

Show no interest? **1 point**

What you need

🐾 Treat

🐾 Timer

Try this long-term memory test too many times and your canine friend might have a bone to pick with you!

1 Make your dog sit (or ask a friend to hold its collar).

2 With your dog watching, hide the treat.

3 Take your dog out of the room and play with it for five minutes.

4 Take your dog back into the room, start the timer and encourage it to find the treat.

When your dog re-enters the room, does it:

Go straight to the treat? **5 points**

Find the treat in 15 seconds? **4 points**

Find the treat in 45 seconds? **3 points**

Fail to find the treat? **2 points**

Show no interest? **1 point**

This exercise will test your dog's ability to solve problems and move objects – and how well it can limbo!

1 With your dog watching, put the treat beneath the table or chair.

2 The table or chair should be low enough so it is difficult for the dog to reach under, but not too low.

3 Start the timer and encourage your dog to get the treat.

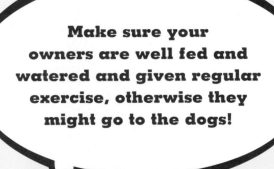

Make sure your owners are well fed and watered and given regular exercise, otherwise they might go to the dogs!

When you encourage your dog, does it:

 Use its paws to get the treat in less than 60 seconds? **5 points**

 Use its paws to get the treat in less then 3 minutes? **4 points**

 Only use its nose to try to get the treat? **3 points**

 Make a couple of attempts to get the treat? **2 points**

 Make no attempt to get the treat? **1 point**

Hero dogs

Whether it's saving lives, braving blizzards, leading people to safety or just being nosy, these dogs know how to perform beyond the call of duty.

When disease threatened to tear through the isolated town of Nome, Alaska, in 1925, the only way to get serum there in time was by sled dog. Leading the final team through darkness and blinding blizzards was Balto, shown here with his driver Gunnar Kaasen.

On a stormy night in December 1919, the SS *Ethie* ran aground on the west coast of Newfoundland. Lifelines were fired from the ship, but failed to reach the shore. Fortunately, a brave Newfoundland dog swam out to grab the line, bring it to land and so save the crew and passengers.

During the attack on the World Trade Center on September 11, 2001, Roselle the Labrador guide dog led her owner, Michael Hingson, down 77 flights of stairs and out of the North Tower to safety.

The first living thing sent into space was a dog! Laika was blasted into orbit on board *Sputnik 2* in November 1957. Sadly, she never returned.

He might not have saved lives, but Trouble the Beagle has prevented other disasters. His work with US Customs has stopped thousands of cases of disease-carrying plants and animals.

The cup trick

What you need

🐾 Treat

🐾 Three paper cups

We might not be the genius of the animal world, but surely we can find a treat under a cup – can't we?

1 Line the paper cups up in front of your dog.

2 Place the treat under one of the cups, while your dog is watching.

3 Turn the dog away for a few seconds, then turn it back and encourage it to find the treat. Make a note of how your dog performs.

Repeat the test and put the treat under the same cup. How long does it take this time?

When you let go of your dog, does it:

Find the treat straight away? **5 points**

Knock over two cups before finding the treat? **4 points**

Knock over three cups before finding the treat? **3 points**

Sniff the cups, but does not knock them over? **2 points**

Make no attempt to find the treat? **1 point**

What you need

🐾 Treats

🐾 Lead

🐾 Chair

Some people say "you can't teach an old dog new tricks". Hopefully, this exercise will prove them wrong...

1 Teach your dog the new trick of circling a chair.

2 Say a command for the trick, guide the dog around the chair and reward it with a treat. Repeat this two more times, leaving a few seconds between each repeat.

3 Now see how many times it takes for your dog to perform the trick on its own.

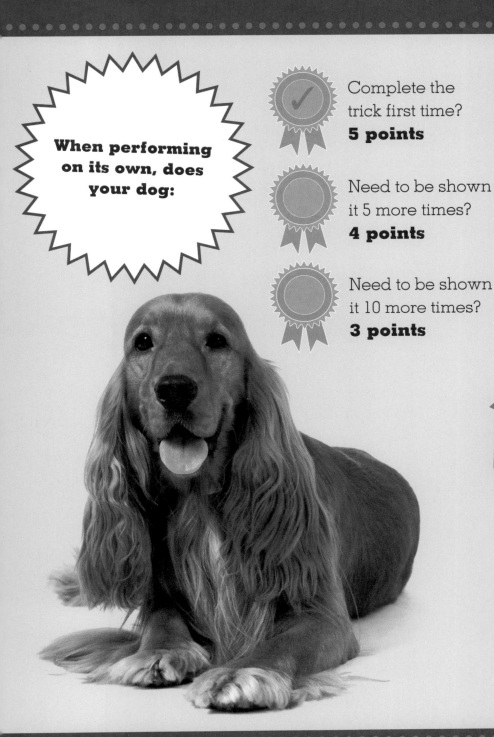

When performing on its own, does your dog:

 Complete the trick first time?
5 points

Need to be shown it 5 more times?
4 points

Need to be shown it 10 more times?
3 points

Need to be shown it 20 more times?
2 points

Fail to perform the trick?
1 point

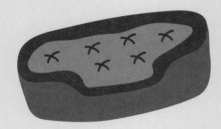

What you need

* Plate
* Two treats

We all know that two treats and two treats equal four treats. But what happens when you have no treats – that's "paws-itively" one unhappy dog!

1 Put the two treats on the plate and hold it in front of your dog so it can see them.

2 Eat one of the treats in one mouthful, closely followed by the second.

3 Note how your dog reacts when you've eaten them both.

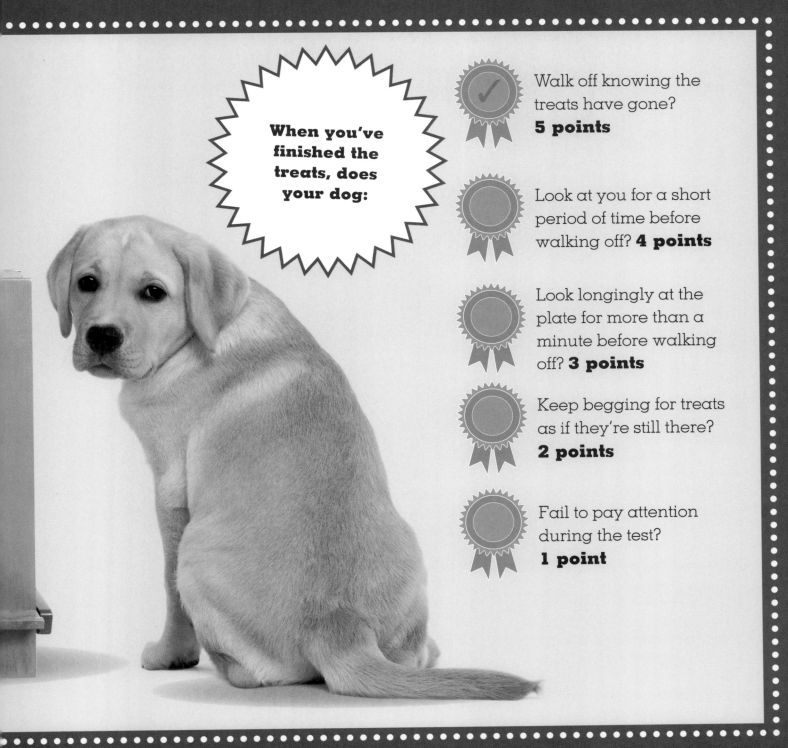

When you've finished the treats, does your dog:

Walk off knowing the treats have gone? **5 points**

Look at you for a short period of time before walking off? **4 points**

Look longingly at the plate for more than a minute before walking off? **3 points**

Keep begging for treats as if they're still there? **2 points**

Fail to pay attention during the test? **1 point**

Good dog!

What you need

🐾 Treat

🐾 Plate

You may think your dog obeys your commands, but we're the ones who are really in control!

1 Place the treat on the plate and leave it where the dog can reach.

2 Leave the room and return after one minute.

3 Repeat this and see if your dog has eaten the treat while you were out.

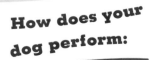 **How does your dog perform:**

 If the dog doesn't take the treat **5 points**

 If the treat goes after three visits **4 points**

 If the treat goes after two visits **3 points**

 If the treat goes after one visit **2 points**

 If your dog eats the treat before you've left the room **1 point**

Having a nice, obedient pet can give you a whole new "leash" of life.

How did they do?

Well, test time is over, so how did your pooch measure up. Add up the scores to find out if you've got a clever canine or a doggy dunce.

Final scores

100-125 Throw a party, your dog's a genius!

50-99 Good going, your dog is better than average!

25-49 There's no gentle way to put this... your dog is dumb – but lovable, right?

Repeat the tests – they may help to improve your pet's reactions, and they'll be fun for the pair of you.

1

2

If your dog shone in all the tests, then congratulations – you've got an Einstein for a pet. Make sure you encourage it to keep up the good work.

Didn't do so well? Then don't worry. Your dog might not be a genius, but you still love it and you can bet that it loves you.

Further information

Books

RSPCA New Complete Dog Training Manual
Fogle, Dr Bruce (DK 2008)

101 Dog Tricks: Step-by-step Activities to Engage, Challenge, and Bond with Your Dog
Sundance, Kyra
(Rockport Publishers 2007)

Dog Training For Dummies
Volhard, Jack and Wendy
(John Wiley & Sons 2010)

My Dog is a Genius: Understand and Improve Your Dog's Intelligence
Taylor, David
(Hamlyn 2008)

The Intelligence of Dogs
Coren, Stanley
(Pocket Books 2006)

100 Ways to Train the Perfect Dog
Fisher, Sarah (David and Charle 2008)

Brain Games For Dogs
Arrowsmith, Claire
(Interpret Publishing 2010)

The Dog Vinci Code
Rogerson, John
(Metro Books 2011)

Train Your Dog Like a Pro
Donaldson, Jean
(John Wiley & Sons 2010)

Websites

www.thedogtrainingclub.com

Hints and tips on training and information on different breeds.

www.thekennelclub.org.uk

Advice on buying, caring and living with dogs.

www.bipdt.org.uk

Home of the British Institute of Professional Dog Trainers.

www.apdt.co.uk

Help with finding a dog trainer and general dog advice.

www.dogstrust.org.uk

Information and advice on breeds and caring for dogs.

www.k9obedience.co.uk

Training and care advice from professional dog handlers.

Index

Acknowledgements

All artworks supplied by The Apple Illustration Agency
Index created by Chris Bernstein

The publishers would like to thank the following for the use of their photographs in the book:

3 Dorottya Mathe, 6–7 WilleeCole, 7tr RamonaS, 8–9 alessandro0770, 8c Pelana, 9tl Eric Isselée, 9b WilleeCole, 10bl WilleeCole, 11l Eric Isselée, 11bl Marina Jay, 12bl Getty Images, 11br Getty Images, 13tl Getty Images, 16bl FotoJagodka, 17bl Hannamariah, 18b Eric Isselée, 20 Erik Lam, 20 Utekhina Anna, 21l Eriklam/Dreamstime.com, 22 Photodisc/Getty Images, 24 RamonaS, 26bl Monika Wisniewska, 28br Lars Christensen, 29tl Susan DeLoach, 29br Rickshu, 30bl Photodisc/Getty Images, 31bl/ Eric Isselée, 31br frotos, 33 Paul Cotney, 33b nito, 35 Peter vd Rol, 36 Dorottya Mathe, 38 Eric Isselée, 41 Zbynek Jirousek, 43 Vitaly Titov & Maria Sidelnikova, 44 Eric Isselée, 45 Jaimie Duplass, 46–47 Erik Lam, 48bl National Geographic/Getty Images, 48tr Bettmann/CORBIS, 49tl Gamma-Rapho via Getty Images, 49br Getty Images, 50 Eric Isselée, 52 Sue McDonald, , 54r Mike Flippo, 54r Picsfive, 55 Eric Isselée, 56 Cheryl Casey, 58b Dorottya Mathe, 59bl robertopalace, 59tr Golden Pixels LLC.